Rock Art

by Vaishali Batra

OXFORD
UNIVERSITY PRESS
AUSTRALIA & NEW ZEALAND

Art on Rocks

Do you like to draw or paint?

Long ago, there was no paper or canvas, pens or pencils. People had to draw on rocks and stones to tell stories about their lives.

This beautiful rock art is at Grapevine Canyon in the United States of America.

Rock art has been discovered in lots of different places around the world. It has been found on mountains, in caves and in the desert.

We are lucky to have rock art because it tells us a lot about history.

These visitors are learning about rock art.

Rock art can be thousands of years old. Some of it is nearly gone because it has faded from the effects of the sun, wind and rain.

This rock art in Queensland, Australia, shows faded kangaroos and dingoes.

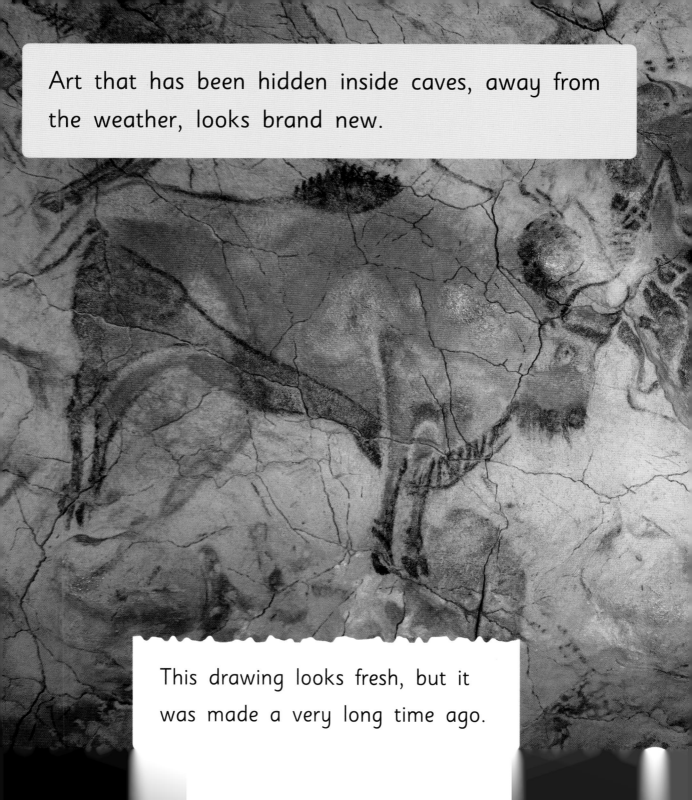

Art that has been hidden inside caves, away from the weather, looks brand new.

This drawing looks fresh, but it was made a very long time ago.

What Does Rock Art Show?

Rock art is a way for us to learn about what people in the past did and what they saw around them.

It shows animals and plants, and activities like growing crops and hunting.

This rock art is from Algeria, in Africa. What animal can you see?

Some rock art is made of handprints or patterns. In Argentina, there is a cave with lots of handprints all over the walls. The prints are over 10 000 years old.

Cave of Hands, Argentina

How Was Rock Art Made?

In the past, people used natural materials to make coloured paint. They crushed and mixed things like **charcoal**, clay, plants and fruit.

Rock art made with paint is called a **pictograph**.

fruit

plants

charcoal

Artists would find sharp stones or break thin sticks to apply paint. They also made brushes with animal feathers and fur.

Tools like these were found in a cave in Spain.

Types of Rock Art

There are lots of other kinds of rock art. Some is made by cutting the rock to show light rock underneath. This is called a **petroglyph**.

This rock art in the United States was made by cutting into the rocks.

When stones are used to make patterns it is called a **petroform**.

This petroform in Canada is in the shape of a turtle.

Rock Art around the World

Namibia, Africa

Thousands of examples of rock art have been
found here at Brandberg Mountain in Namibia.
Some are more than 25 000 years old.

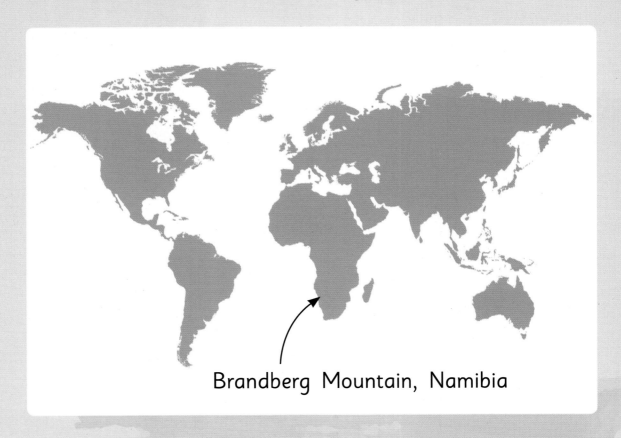

Brandberg Mountain, Namibia

The rock art on Brandberg Mountain shows how people hunted and gathered their food. There are also pictures that show how people dressed.

Can you imagine what these people looked like?

Australia

Kakadu National Park is in the Northern Territory, Australia. It has three rock art sites. Some of the art is over 20000 years old.

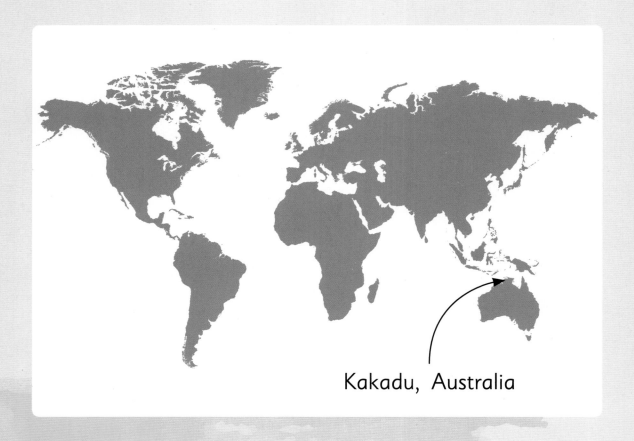

Kakadu, Australia

Some rock drawings at Kakadu have the outline of a person or animal and you can see bones, muscles and **organs**.

This type of rock art is called **X-ray art**.

Aboriginal people use art to show their close relationship with the land or to tell stories.

There are many stories and art about the Rainbow Serpent. The Rainbow Serpent is linked to water and the seasons.

This rock art near Kakadu honours the story of the Rainbow Serpent.

India

A large collection of rock art was found in caves in central India. There are over 100 paintings and some are more than 10000 years old.

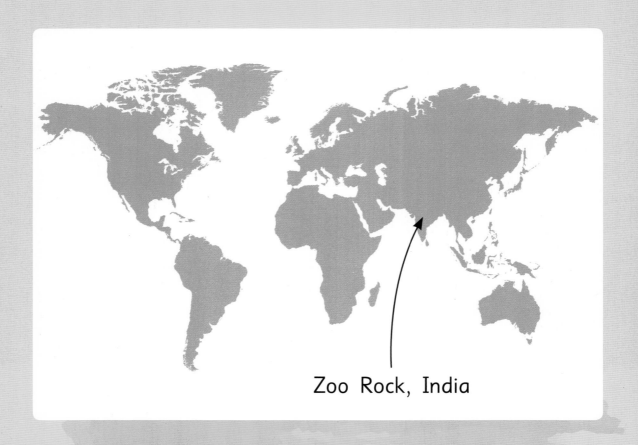

Zoo Rock, India

The cave paintings in India show different aspects of life.

Lots of people lived in and around these caves over time. Some of the art has been painted over with new pictures.

The paintings are mostly in red and white. Some show people singing and dancing, while others show people hunting.

This painting from the caves in India shows **warriors** preparing to go to war.

A well-known part of the Indian caves is called Zoo Rock. The rock is decorated with drawings of nearly 200 animals, including deer, antelope and elephants.

These animals were painted on the roof of the cave.

A Picture Book of the Past

Rock art lets us imagine the lives of people who lived thousands of years ago. It tells us how people found food, what they looked like and what activities they did.

The art lets us see the world through their eyes.

What story would your rock art tell?

Glossary

charcoal: a black substance made by burning wood slowly

organs: parts of the body that have a function

petroform: shapes and patterns made by lining up large rocks on the ground

petroglyph: a drawing on rock made by cutting the rock

pictograph: a drawing or painting on rock

warriors: people who fight in battles

X-ray art: a drawing or painting that shows the inside of the body

Index